Hacking Growth

Alex Kehr

FOR MY MOM

CONTENTS

Assume nobody else has any idea what they're doing, either.
- Aaron Swartz

FOREWORD

I built my first website when I was 9 years old. I was in the fourth grade, in the computer lab at Marquez Elementary Charter School in the Pacific Palisades. The website was just a collection of GIFs of Pokémon exploding and I built it using the now defunct Homepage.com. The moment after creating my first website I was hooked on the Internet. I immediately saw how I could come up with an idea, bring it to life, and deliver my idea to people around the globe almost instantaneously. That Pokémon GIF site was the beginning of my passion for the Internet and its ability to make the boundaries of knowledge and ideas limitless.

I built many other websites after that initial project on Homepage.com, and eventually became proficient at HTML (by the time fourth grade was over). Around fifth grade, AOL Instant Messenger (AIM) became huge. I was bummed that I couldn't get a good screen name because all of the good names were taken and eventually found myself in a weird online community of teen "hackers" who were stealing AIM screen names and reselling them. I'd discovered the AIM screen name black market (yes, this was a real thing), and was mesmerized by it. I downloaded Visual Studio and taught myself C++. With my very basic C++ knowledge I was able to build myself password-cracking software. I figured out how to connect to the AIM proxy servers, type in the screen name I wanted, and load in massive password lists. Once I had these three variables entered into my program, I hit "Go" and was able to test thousands of passwords. If a successful connection was made with a screen name and password combination, the screen name and password were saved into a text file. I would then log in to the accounts and change the passwords to make the names mine. If I didn't want a screen name, I would sell it on eBay or on a forum (this all happened around sixth grade).

Towards the end of the sixth grade, I exited this "teen hacker" phase and discovered Counter Strike. I played a lot of Counter Strike and eventually wanted to make my own servers (online multiplayer gaming environment). I purchased my own server, which I paid around $70 per month for, and created "Slinky's Assault Server" (Slinky was my gamer tag). My server became immensely popular and was always filled with Counter Strike players from all around the world. I saw this as a great opportunity to have people pay for my server for me, so I allowed a handful of people to pay to be an admin. People from Canada, Germany, and a few other countries were paying me $10 to $20 per month to manage my server for me.

I realized that with more servers, I could offer web hosting to people too. I piggybacked off the success of my Counter Strike server and created a web hosting company called Nodus Hosting. I was around 13 or 14 years old at this time, and had created a pretty viable business. I had about 150 customers paying me anywhere from $5 to $50 per month, and I went as far as purchasing a 1-800 phone number that went directly to my bedroom so that I could offer customer support.

Having 150 customers proved to be difficult for me at 14 years old, so I decided to find a company that had similar values to mine and give them my customers.

After my web hosting company and Counter Strike servers no longer existed, I took a little break from creating any real online projects. However, this break ended August of 2005 when something popped up on the news and caught my attention: Hurricane Katrina. I saw that a lot of people were going to be displaced and homeless, so I stayed up all night to program and design a website called FindKatrina. After building the website, I had no idea how to get people to actually use it. I decided to go to Craigslist and post on the New Orleans page that my site, FindKatrina, existed. I went to bed after posting the site, and when I woke up the storm was devastating the Gulf Coast. People saw my Craigslist post overnight and started posting their virtual flyers for missing friends and family members with instructions on how to get in contact with each other on my website. Thousands of people made postings on the site, and this was only fueled by publications such as *WIRED* and The *New York Time*s writing about me and the website. This was a turning point for me because it taught me how simple, creative, and abstract marketing could make a website an overnight success. It also taught me that I could have a meaningful impact on the world by building out my ideas on the Internet.

I have created plenty of other successful websites besides just FindKatrina, but I'm going to end the *history of me* there. The story of my passion for the Internet evolving highlights my consistent ability to make something out of nothing online, while also showing how I developed the hacker mentality at an early age. The brief story of the creation my first website to building FindKatrina provides a peek into why I have a distinctively imaginative worldview and workflow.

My uniquely imaginative way of looking at the world is what leads me to the primary goal of this book: inspire you, ignite your brain, and remind you that marketing is the perfect mixture of business and creativity (which I think makes it one of the most exciting professions out there). We will accomplish these goals by focusing on marketing tactics that have been dubbed "growth hacking." Growth hacking is a marketing mindset, largely used by startups, to come up with creative and low-cost marketing tactics using data and analytical thinking to grow a business efficiently. A growth hacker uses their aspirational attitude and understanding of data to do one thing much more efficiently than a traditional marketer: hack growth.

Throughout this book, we will examine ways that you can hack growth to achieve impressive business results and have the most fun you've ever had building a business. I decided to structure the book in a way that explains what it means to be a growth hacker, provide lessons from companies that successfully grew fast using unconventional growth tactics, and help guide you towards success by hopefully inspiring you to come up with creative and fun ideas that will help you build a business that triumphs.

CHAPTER 1
WHAT IS A GROWTH HACKER?

A growth hacker inhabits an area of business where data, product, and marketing collide. A growth hacker breaks down the barrier between marketing and product teams by helping to create product features that have marketing baked into them. A growth hacker has a plan not just to sell more to each customer, but also give each customer more reasons to talk about a company (and make it easy to talk about and share a product). A growth hacker thinks about marketing as a strategy for growth, not just sales – they mix SEO, social media, community building, content marketing, brand development, and analytics. A growth hacker recognizes that it is really hard to build a company, and comes up with easier, faster, and cheaper ways to help craft successful businesses.

What does growth hacking look like in practice?

A growth hacker is a technical thinking marketer who has the ability to ask difficult questions when tasked with making a product *go viral*. A growth hacker knows that making a product *go viral* means asking a customer to talk about a product, for free. Asking a customer to talk about a product, for free, is a huge request because by asking a customer to share your product, you're asking a customer to spend his or her social capital to help you grow a business. A growth hacker approaches the task of growing a business fast by first asking questions along the lines of: "Is our product remarkable enough to share? If our product is remarkable enough to share, have we made it easy enough for our customer to share it? What will motivate our customers to talk about us? What are the benefits to our customers for talking about us?"

These types of questions from a growth hacker are tremendously valuable because making something *go viral* doesn't miraculously happen since virality isn't an accident: it is engineered. Virality has to be meticulously planned since asking somebody to spend his or her social capital to share something that you're working on, for free, is a huge request. When you're asking your customer things along the lines of, "Post about me on Facebook or Twitter," you're asking them for a favor. Instead of making it sound like the customer is lending you a hand, it's more beneficial to position your request as if you aren't asking for a favor by giving a user value for sharing. Helping your customer increase his or her social standing within his or her circle of friends by making it cool to talk about a product will go a long way. You need to be able to provoke a desire in people to spread something. People aren't going to organically share something unless it's truly remarkable and worth sharing.

Growth hackers make things shareable and remarkable. Dropbox is one of the best growth hacker marketing examples because they had incredible growth results and built their company on people recommending their product to each other. Their "Get free space" button was what sparked their monumental growth. If you've ever used Dropbox, you've probably seen that button. The "Get free space" button led to an offer for free file storage space, but you only got the free file storage space when you invited a friend to Dropbox and got them to sign up. This, almost immediately, caused Dropbox signups to accelerate to 60 percent higher[1], with these growth levels staying constant for months after the referral program began. This program was insanely effective and led to over 2.8 million direct invites per month[2]. That is some seriously impressive growth and referral program engagement.

What Dropbox did is different than traditional marketing because instead of expecting a marketing person to magically make a product *go viral*, a growth hacker helped craft the way the product worked and was presented to the users, all with the intent of making the Dropbox product more shareable. Instead of being given a product to sell like a traditional marketer, a growth hacker helps create products that sell themselves.

To reinforce these notions, you can't just do things

like make a YouTube video about whatever you want and expect it to get 10 million views, or expect users to become diehard evangelists of products— users need to be provided incentives to become evangelists and be given the resources to easily spread the word.

The role of the growth hacker is to creatively incentivize customers to promote a brand, for free (or as close to free as possible). When customers promote your brand for you, the foundation of a powerful brand community is being laid out.

The future of marketing is growth hacking

While most marketing roles won't officially label a person a "growth hacker," the growth hacker mentality is the future of marketing. If you can harness the growth hacker mentality before it is mainstream marketing, you will be a powerful growth weapon for your company. Embracing unconventional growth tactics and the growth hacker mentality is what has helped companies such as Airbnb, Dropbox, Uber, and other quick growing startups achieve exceptionally fast and enormous growth.

A growth hacker is a marketer who figures out how to achieve growth without expensive traditional marketing methods and also often figures out how to piggyback off successful platforms like Facebook, Twitter, and Google to grow. To accomplish growth, a growth hacker disregards the traditional marketing routine and replaces it with a set of practices that are distinctively testable and scalable. A great growth hacker comes up with methods to use content marketing, APIs, email lists, social networks, smart pay-per-click ad purchasing, and other less conventional marketing tactics as primary marketing methods. A growth hacker is a marketer who doesn't necessarily see value in throwing money at television commercials or paying PR companies to try to get them press because they are confident that they can make growth happen faster, with higher quality users, using their ultra-creative and somewhat scrappy marketing approach.

Because building a growth marketing plan means throwing out the traditional marketing playbook, it is vital that you can easily explain your growth model to anybody that asks. If you can't simply explain what you're doing (or going to do) to grow a company, it's most likely too complex of an idea and won't work. Create a simple and distinctive growth strategy that you can easily explain, around a meaningful experience, and you've found your way down a brilliant growth path.

Why do we call it growth *hacking*?

We call this type of marketing growth *hacking* because it embraces the hacker mentality. The hacker mentality involves a core set of values: a radical belief in the impossible, an antiestablishment disposition, and a deep desire to conquer difficult problems using "technological and social solutions, and an almost religious belief in the power of data to aid in solving those problems[3]."

Growth hackers are dedicated problem solvers who are interested in discovering holes in systems as they currently exist and exploiting them for intellectual, creative, and business gain. By identifying weaknesses in long-established systems, growth hackers have successfully disrupted countless industries, from retail and music to transportation and publishing[3]. A great growth hacker, like the stereotypical troublemaker hacker, is more interested in executing on their ideas than making massive amounts of money. However, unlike the stereotypical hacker, a growth hacker has the ultimate goal of being an empire builder, but isn't necessarily focused on the monetary gain part of building an empire. A growth hacker simply wants to change the world by flexing their creative muscle.

A growth hacker is focused

Focus is vital when it comes to growth hacking, and the boundary of staying focused on your primary goals will make you reach your maximum creative potential. You can't win at growth marketing if you aren't extremely focused on your intended outcome. The need to be immensely focused is why you need to make goals that force you to be focused on the marketing activities that return the most value for the time you've invested, and you need to be able to prioritize goals. Your highest priority goals need to remain at the top of your mind, and you need to be able to ignore lower priority goals that steal your time away from your higher priority goals.

You will win at growth marketing if you stay focused. Your focus will allow you to move faster, learn faster, progress faster, build confidence, and help you discover your competitive advantage[4]:

1. Move faster: Focus will allow you to create a less complex marketing strategy, which means you can make smarter decisions more quickly. When it's easier to make decisions, you can progress your business at a faster rate than when you have to make hard decisions.

2. Learn faster: When you can move faster, and make decisions more quickly, you learn more.

3. Progress faster: You will be able to progress faster when you are both moving faster and learning faster. When you progress faster because you're moving fast and learning fast, your business will grow faster.

4. Build confidence: You will build confidence in your business faster when you see it progress faster. When confidence is obvious, the team building a company will feel even more motivated

to build a lasting business and push their professional boundaries.

5. <u>Discover your competitive advantage</u>: When you're focused, you become really good at a few things faster, which means you can discover your competitive advantage faster. When you clearly know what you're better at than your competitors you can develop a marketing strategy that truly allows your business to grow.

One of the biggest advantages to being focused is that it's going to be easier to notice when something works. When you notice something works, you know it's time to scale that growth experiment and craft your killer growth marketing strategy around it.

CHAPTER 2
CREATING YOUR KILLER GROWTH MARKETING STRATEGY

When crafting your killer marketing strategy, you should keep a few fundamental ideas in mind: you need to remember to define your target audience, set clear goals, and address competitor weaknesses. If you remember to do those three things, there's no reason why you shouldn't be able to successfully grow your business.

Defining your target audience:

Defining whom you're aiming your marketing efforts

at is an extremely important aspect when it comes to creating smart marketing campaigns. This step is oddly often forgotten by a lot of marketers and company founders because ambitious people frequently target everybody, hoping that some people will listen and turn into customers. This is no different than playing darts by grabbing a handful of darts and throwing them all at the dartboard at once, hoping that one dart hits the board as a bullseye. If you take the time to focus on the bullseye, rather than aim at everything, your focus will pay off and you'll be able to create a message that resonates with your target audience and drives the biggest results possible. Take some time to think about the pain point your product or service is solving for your target audience, and build a strategy that your target audience can relate to best.

Set clear goals:

You need goals to be successful. If you don't have goals, you have nothing to reach for and no way to evaluate how successful your marketing efforts are. Spend some time thinking about what you're trying to accomplish and set goals that are difficult, yet attainable. If you're building up an email list, you might set a modest goal of getting 250 email signups in a month. If you have just created your company a Facebook page, maybe you want to get 1,000 page likes in three months. Think about your goals each day and figure out if your current efforts are helping you reach what you've set out to accomplish. If things aren't working, try new things, and if things are working, think about how to scale and refine what works.

Address competitor weaknesses:

Every company has weaknesses in their marketing strategy, and it's the job of a competitor to scout the weaknesses out and pounce. A great example of how you might do this is evaluating your competitors and noticing that they all have bad content marketing efforts. If you notice that your competitions content marketing efforts are weak, you can use this as an opportunity to create great content that makes your brand more credible and trustworthy than them. When your brand is positioned as being more credible and trustworthy than a competitor's brand, you're going to win over more customers than your competition and be better positioned to build a healthier long-term business.

Every brilliant marketing strategy is rooted in taking advantage of competitor weaknesses, setting goals, and defining your target audience. If you think about these three things when crafting a marketing strategy, you're instantly on the way to being more successful with your marketing efforts.

After taking the time to define your target audience, set clear goals, and address competitor weaknesses, you're ready to think about the *growth hacker conversion funnel*[1]. We call what we are about to discuss the growth hacker funnel because a funnel has a big opening at the top and the hole becomes smaller and smaller as we go lower down the funnel. A funnel guides a lot of liquid down a narrow path and then the liquid exits out to exactly where we want it to go. The way liquid moves down a funnel is a relevant analogy when thinking about growth marketing. It's relevant because it's the growth hackers mission to get people into the top of the funnel and then guide them towards accomplishing the particular goal that they have in mind. The goal can be anything from a mailing list signup, a checkout (sale), filling out a contact form, to really just about anything that helps a business grow. A well-thought-out funnel lets you take out the unpredictability of people using your product and you can more easily get people to take the actions that you want them to take. A growth marketer is looking to make a significant amount of people enter at the top of the funnel and then guide them down a set path to the bottom of the funnel. To better understand the growth funnel, we can break it down into three stages: get visitors, activate members, and retain users[1].

The very top of the growth funnel is the "get visitors" stage. This is simply you getting people to visit your website, ideally for the first time. We call people visitors at this initial stage of the funnel because they haven't converted yet. People at this stage of the funnel haven't done any of the actions you want them to do yet and you don't yet have a meaningful relationship with them. These people are essentially strangers, they're just visitors, and it is your job to make them feel comfortable with you because you are also a stranger to them. When the visitor feels comfortable with your company or product, worthwhile progress has happened on the marketing front.

Once the visitor feels comfortable with the product, you can start to activate the visitor and focus on turning them into a member. You can think of this point of the funnel as you having gone on a great first date and you are now ready to take things to the next level and enter into a relationship (you like to move things fast!).

Taking this next step forward in the growth funnel is hard. You achieve the step forward from visitor to member once a person has done an action that you've set out to make them do. This could be a wide array of things: buying something from you, creating a free account, joining your mailing list, following your social media accounts, to really whatever goal that you feel is beneficial to your business objectives.

When somebody has done something like make a purchase or joins your email list, they have become a member— you've entered into a relationship with each other. Now that you've gotten your visitor to become a member, it's time to think about the final stage of the growth funnel: making them a retained user.

A retained user is a person who uses your product with regular frequency. A retained user is a person who sticks around for a fair amount of time and loves using your product. A retained user is what every growth marketer seeks, and the more retained users you can get, the more successful you are as a growth hacker.

CHAPTER 3
CREATING A STRONG COMMUNITY

Community is the core of every great business and every great growth hacker marketing success story. This is why before we talk about some clever growth marketing tactics that you can use, we first have to recognize the importance of being community-driven with all of your marketing. This is because you build the best modern companies by focusing on growing a strong community. A strong community will do almost all of the legwork for you when it comes to getting new people to visit your product (then it's your job to send them down the funnel!).

The best modern companies are built by focusing on growing communities because it's arguably impossible to scale a product or business without building a community around it. When you build a strong community early on, you accomplish two fantastic things for your business: (1) you build traction and fuel growth because early users often become the best product evangelists and (2) you better position your business for long-term success because your community will want to see you grow and succeed, and do everything in their power to help you thrive.

Building a great community can seem like a pretty daunting task, but it's really not too bad of a task to conquer. There are three things that you can do early on that will help you achieve meaningful growth and gain traction on the community building front. These three things are: establish a mission, encourage your community to share with one another, and talk to your audience.

Establish a mission: This might be one of the most important things that a business can do, that a lot fail at doing. A business that actively shows they are about more than just making money will have an easier time growing than a company that is obviously focused only on the bottom line. A mission-driven company builds a strong community, which positions it for long-term success. When your business stands for something, your users (and potential users) feel that when they use your product or service they are part of something bigger than themselves. A strong mission gives people a shared sense of purpose when they're part of a community, incentivizing them to help grow your community (at no cost to your business).

Encourage your community to share with one another: You should be encouraging your users to connect with each other, making them feel like they're part of a community that clicks and comes up with ideas to make your company stronger, together.

Talk to your audience: Community members love to hear from the company. Take time to connect with the people who love your brand most, and let them know that they're valued. Sending gifts and emails to these customers is a good start, but personal interactions are much more powerful. Personal interactions are more powerful because once you've met face-to-face, and have shared a laugh or drink together, the relationship is going to last forever. Physical/offline events are the best opportunities for you to meet and connect with users, while introducing them to your company.

There are also two added bonuses from focusing on community at the beginning of your businesses life:

1. When you talk to your audience you'll be able to create better products. Your most dedicated evangelists will be able to honestly tell you what they like and dislike about your product because they want to see you succeed. You're more likely to create a great product because you get important user feedback early on.

2. Community building helps with recruiting. When you have a passionate community of people who want your product to succeed, you've effectively created a brilliant talent pool for your business. When your hires come from your community, they're going to have a clear, shared vision for success and do everything they can to be insanely successful in their role because they passionately believe in your company mission.

Initial key takeaways when thinking about community building:

1. Smart companies build strong communities. Strong communities build strong companies.

2. Strong communities are created by evangelists who believe in your company mission.

3. Encourage members to communicate with each other (at events, on your website, etc.).

4. Focus on the quality of your community early on. Keep it positive and fun so people want to continue coming back and contributing.

5. Community building often helps you gain traction because you find people who believe in your mission and vocally help you become more successful.

It's hard to stress just how important it is to build an outstanding community early on. Let's first identify how early growth marketing comes down to avoiding investing too much time in certain activities that don't really matter. When you're too focused on the things that don't matter, you forget about concentrating on the marketing activities that pose the most significant barriers to you gaining traction. We want to recognize this because it reminds us that when you have a strong community, you can share ideas with them and they can help you predict the outcome of marketing activities. When you can accurately predict the outcome of marketing activities because of your community, you can avoid spending too much time and money on potentially ineffective ideas.

A lot of startups have an "if you build it, they will come" mentality. This mentality can be deadly, and it's important to think about how nobody is going to use your product if they don't believe in your brand. Your brand is more than just a name or logo, but it's the personality of your business. Having a strong brand is a vital part of a strong business. When people believe in your brand, they're going to care about your success. When people care about your success, they share the value they receive from your product with people they know *because they'll want to see you thrive.*

To make people believe in your brand, you should be creating high quality branded content early on. Creating content can be time consuming, but that's OK because it doesn't make sense to focus on the scalability of your marketing efforts when people haven't even learned about your brand at all yet. Good early marketing will automatically scale well, as long as you focus on creating content that is highly targeted and does a fantastic job demonstrating your value proposition and company mission in an effective manner. A lot of people try to grow their marketing before they even understand their market— this is a huge mistake that's fairly easy to avoid.

To avoid trying to scale your marketing efforts before you properly understand your market, you can do a few things early on that will allow you to better understand your market and build a community around your company:

1. <u>Meet people</u>. Don't market from behind your computer. Go to events and have real conversations with the people you meet about how your company is going to help them solve a problem.

2. Create and share content that is relevant to your target customer. By sharing and creating content, you're position yourself as a trustworthy expert. Just make sure that you don't have any typos or bad grammar because either of those mistakes in your content marketing efforts will immediately throw any credibility you've gained out of the window.

3. Become a familiar face at events relevant to your target customer. When you're on the top of your target customers' mind, you're at the tip of their tongue— when the people you keep meeting at relevant events have the problem you're solving, they'll come to you first.

These tactics do more than just educate your target customer about you, but they actually educate you too. When you're creating content and going to events, you're learning even more about the industry you're trying to help. This will take your expertise to another level. Ultra high quality content and face-to-face moments with your target audience are essential for building your community.

Your community will allow you to create an extremely loyal customer base. The Wharton School of the University of Pennsylvania published a great article on their *Knowledge@Wharton* blog about how the digital marketing landscape is rapidly changing. The rules of marketing are changing and, according to a panel of experts who spoke at the 2014 Wharton Marketing Conference, need to focus on creating personal connections rather than sending out random Tweets and Facebook posts.

"It is rather ironic. We have more data than ever before, but the overwhelming evidence is that customer loyalty is lower[1]," said Chris Malone, managing partner at Fidelum Partners, who took part in a panel called *Building Loyal Customers in the Information Age*. Malone continued by explaining that previously "commerce was face to face, as much about the person, the relationship you had with him and what you stood for. Data can be a great tool to rebuild that. [But] you have to show that the customer is not just another cookie on the browser[1]."

What it really seems to come down to is making people feel part of a community by being authentic.

Vanessa Rosado, global director of digital capabilities for AB InBev, elaborated on this: "If you have been authentic, consumers will love you and share your brand[1]."

Creating a strong community is how you get the most visitors. The more people that visit your product, the more opportunities you have to get customers. A strong community also means that the customers you create are most likely to be retained and are highly likely to be extremely passionate about your product and will want to be a part of helping it succeed. With a strong community, your customers will be incredibly loyal, and feel a deep desire to help your business grow and prosper.

Vimeo's community:

I was one of the very first members of Vimeo, a video sharing website that competes with YouTube. I was member number 30 or so, and when I joined on June 14, 2005 I had to e-mail Jake Lodwick (one of the founders) asking for an account because there was no signup page yet. Being a member of Vimeo very early on allowed me to see one of the most creative websites on the Internet come to life, and I undoubtedly helped build its strong community (even though I didn't realize it at the time). There were just a few of us uploading videos when I joined, but we were commenting on everything being uploaded and encouraging one another to go on creative adventures. The encouraging atmosphere of Vimeo made all of us extremely loyal because we felt a deep desire to explore our creative boundaries and share our artistic discoveries with the Vimeo community. Besides being encouraged to push ourselves creatively as early members of Vimeo, the staff was constantly interacting with us and they built every feature with our feedback.

(continued on next page)

In fact, I was able to dig up my very first private message on the site. It was from Vimeo co-founder Jake Lodwick asking me to look at a beta version of a major update to Vimeo:

My Messages with Jake Lodwick ALUM

 Jake Lodwick ALUM 9 years ago
let me know what you think of this: **vimeo.com/v4**
it's in progress still...

This type of inclusion into the actual building of the site, not just being a person uploading videos, made me amazingly loyal to Vimeo and I shared the site with as many people as possible. I wasn't just loyal to Vimeo, I passionately wanted to see it succeed and went out of my way to do what I could to try to help make it successful.

CHAPTER 4
LOYALTY

Marketing today is all about loyalty. Loyalty is one of the most important aspects of marketing today because it means that a product has been crafted into something that customers believe in and will also tell other people about it. A growth hacker focuses intensely on turning a customer into a loyal customer. When a customer is loyal, he or she is willing to spend their social capital telling people how great you are, which means the people they are referring are much more likely to purchase your product and become active users. Loyalty is a cycle, and it is the responsibility of the growth hacker to conquer the loyalty cycle to achieve full growth potential.

McKinsey & Company, a major worldwide management consulting firm, has created a model that they believe best describes the customer relationship and experience with a brand. Their model takes into account that even after a purchase is made, a customer will continue interacting with a brand. These continued interactions with a company impact a customer's loyalty in both positive and negative ways.[1]

The beginning of loyalty all starts with a trigger that tells the customer that a certain brand or product is even a consideration (the top of the growth hacker funnel). When a product or brand enters consideration, the customer starts to evaluate the brand as a viable option for their needs. This could lead to shopping around for similar products and seeing if you satisfy what they're looking for. The shopping around phase is also a reminder of the value of community. A strong community is likely to refer people to you, and peer-to-peer referral is going to help you get a customer to convert because somebody who they trust has referred them to your product (and the potential new customer probably won't shop around at all if a friend refers them). However, even a high quality referral, which turns into a customer, will lead to a customer that is continuously reevaluating their decision to keep using a brand.

A customer will keep reevaluating their decision to keep using a brand because the customer experience goes well beyond the initial purchase, which can impact long-term loyalty. Just because a person needs what you offer doesn't mean they are going to keep using you. A person may not continue using you because a wide variety of variables can impact a customer's choice to use your product repeatedly. A competitor could introduce better packaging than you, have lower prices and a similar quality product, or have had a positive or negative customer service experience with your company. If anything has hurt a customer's enjoyment of a product, there is a risk of losing their loyalty.

The model that McKinsey & Company has created is called the loyalty loop, and it makes it easy to understand the consumer decision journey:

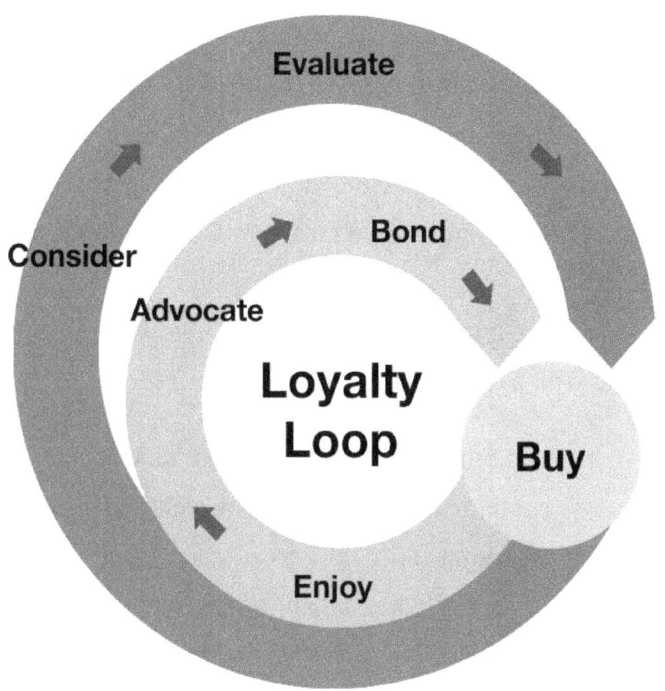

There is a lot to be learned from the loyalty loop. It helps a growth hacker think about and manage the ongoing customer experience. It also helps the growth hacker come up with a content supply chain, which is a consistent set of messages delivered to customers that continuously validates that they've made the right decisions by using your product or service— and are making the right decision staying loyal to it.

With this in mind, a growth marketing professional needs to remember that every time a customer interacts with a brand they need to be receiving a clear and confident message. This helps reduce the likeliness that a customer will realize they better identify with another brand, decide they don't want to use your product anymore, or confuse your brand with a competitor's brand.

Including the loyalty loop into your marketing strategy, combined with constant consideration as to how well you are tackling the growth hacking funnel and your community building efforts, is the ultimate way to set a foundation for brand and product success. However, to accomplish success, you're probably going to stumble a few times and failure is something that doesn't need to be feared. You can use failure to grow. That's why in chapter 5 we are going to talk about making mistakes to succeed fast.

CHAPTER 5
MAKING MISTAKES FAST TO SUCCEED

Be wrong as fast as you can because quick failures are the best learning opportunities. This idea can be difficult for some to grasp because most people don't want to fail. But, if you fail fast and fail early, you're going to learn quickly and ultimately be a better innovator and growth hacker. You become more innovative when you aren't afraid of failure because failing is a direct result of bending the implications of what you thought you knew. Failure comes from taking risks and it changes your understanding of reality.

Failure comes from experimentation, and experiments are effectively fact-finding missions. When you do an experiment you risk failure, which is a great thing because an experiment produces new information and moves you closer to a better understanding of your eventual goal. If your initial theory is wrong, that's OK because you're now armed with new facts that allow you to reframe your initial question and move closer to success, faster.

Embracing the idea of failure as being acceptable is going to lead you (and your company) to be less afraid of taking risks. This is important because when you become too opposed to taking risks, you're going to stop innovating and start rejecting new ideas. Pixar co-founder Ed Catmull wrote in his book, *Creativity, Inc.*, that being too risk-averse is the first step down a path towards irrelevance. He added that to be a sincerely creative company, you need to start trying and doing things that might fail.[1]

Growing from failure

There are two parts to any failure: there is the actual event of failing, and then there is the reaction to the failure. Instead of falling and ignoring what you tripped on, you should step back and assess the situation and grow creatively and professionally. To grow creatively and professionally from failure, you need to discuss your failure and its effects. This is more than just an academic exercise, but an exercise that gives you a better understanding of what exactly what went wrong. Unfortunately, discussing failure can be very difficult to do because people are often afraid of discussing what they did wrong. If you're running a company, you should knock down this barrier of fear and create an atmosphere in which making mistakes doesn't make employees feel humiliated. Allowing employees to fail will develop them and help them grow into much stronger team members and contributors to your company.

Why failing matters

When it comes to failure, let people in your company know that it is perfectly acceptable to make mistakes (or help your boss understand the importance of this). More importantly, let people fix their mistakes so that they can learn from them to become more creative and better at their role within your company. If you aren't ever failing, you are making a mistake that is far worse for a business: being driven by the desire to avoid doing something wrong. When you're driven by the idea of avoiding failure, you aren't taking any risks, which means that you aren't being innovative. Playing it safe and taking no risks means you're accepting the status quo and it'll be nearly impossible to thrive in a quickly changing business landscape. A growth hacker will find that she or he can't be successful if they fear failing.

CHAPTER 6
BUILDING YOUR BRAND

The previous chapter about failure may have seemed somewhat random, but it actually does serve a meaningful purpose. Its purpose is to remind us that experimentation is how we learn and how we grow. In the case of growth marketing, we can take what we learn from experimentation and failure to build a powerful brand. Rapid experimentation allows us to quickly uncover the messaging that resonates best with visitors and converts those visitors to members, and then to retained users.

A modern brand is successful when it is built on a foundation that empowers consumers. Previously, marketing was driven by brands that were able to push their messaging through traditional channels like television, newspaper, and magazines. But, today, the consumer controls the brand. Brands are now consumer-driven and it's important that a company remembers this to avoid becoming irrelevant. Consumers can now find exactly the information they want on a brand, which means they can get only the information that's helpful to them. They can now often cut through the thought-out brand messaging and quickly determine if a product satisfies what they're looking for. This brings us back to the power of a community around a brand. A strong community is going to be writing positive reviews about your product and telling their friends and family about your product. This is hugely advantageous for a business because it means that while a potential new customer is doing research on your product, they're going to have a positive notion of you in their mind because somebody they trust told them about your product, or they're going to feel comfortable with you when they stumble on tons of positive reviews. That being said, traditional marketing still matters, but a smart company recognizes that it must move past purely focusing on traditional marketing communication methods and come up with creative ways to turn customers into evangelists who spread your brand's message.

This is relationship marketing, and a smart modern brand needs to be really good at it. A brand that is doing a great job with relationship marketing is positioning itself for long-term success because it's helping demonstrate long-term value. By demonstrating long-term value, customer satisfaction and retention will increase.

Hotels and airlines have found success on the relationship marketing front by offering financial benefits for remaining loyal. Airlines have their frequent flyer programs that reward frequent flyers with free trips and added benefits, while most hotels also allow you to accumulate points and give frequent guests room upgrades. These types of programs are great, but they're also very traditional. In addition to offering financial benefits to the relationship, a modern-day brand will add in social referral benefits.

We briefly talked about Dropbox in chapter 1, but

it's worth taking a more in-depth look at how they achieved massive growth using relationship marketing that benefited users financially by incentivizing them to share their product. The marketers at Dropbox had a realization early on that led them to find their growth engine: they identified that one of the most powerful channels for user acquisition was their existing users. They came to this conclusion because they understood that word-of-mouth advertising could accelerate their growth by having friends recommend using a product to each other. This realization led Dropbox to introduce their incentivized invite program.

The idea of an incentive program wasn't new, but Dropbox just happened to do a brilliant job implementing their program. What made Dropbox's incentive program so compelling was that everywhere you looked on the Dropbox web interface you were constantly reminded that you should invite more friends to use Dropbox. Users of Dropbox quickly learned that they would get more storage space if they invited friends, and the additional 500MB being offered per referral was a very compelling amount. The storage bonus from Dropbox was an offer that users didn't just want, but often needed. If a person ran out of space and wasn't ready to pay, they just had to find a friend to join Dropbox to get more space. This was a fantastic incentive because it is something that every user of Dropbox could find attractive. Another factor that likely made the Dropbox incentive program work so well is that users saw the benefit of their referral immediately. Dropbox users could simply get one referral signup and they would start getting more space instantly—they didn't need to invite multiple people to start seeing the benefits for the referral incentive program. By immediately showing the benefits to the user, Dropbox was able to demonstrate that referring people was worth the effort.

Dropbox could have ended their referral program there, but they decided to take the time to figure out how to make it addictive. They accomplished this by sending out a simple email with the subject "Dropbox referral status." This was sent immediately upon a referred user creating an account. The email did a fantastic job reengaging Dropbox users because the subject was a simple hook, and once the email was opened the user was reminded how much space they had available for use and how of much space they had just earned for referring somebody. But, in addition to the space reminder, the email reminded people that they should invite even more users to get even more space. The email was a digital high five that reminded you of your successful referral and encouraged you to try to earn even more space while you were still savoring the high of the previous referral.

One of the greatest parts of the Dropbox referral program was that it didn't really cost Dropbox anything. It cost Dropbox almost nothing to implement their referral program because the amount of space that a user saw that they had available was simply a number in a database— it wouldn't cost Dropbox anything until a user actually started using their newly earned storage. Most Dropbox users get nowhere near their maximum storage capacity, so this immensely successful program was extremely cost effective.

Dropbox did a brilliant job enticing people to earn more space, figuring out how to reengage users, and get new users at an extremely low price. They crafted a simple growth hacking strategy that didn't use traditional marketing methods. By ditching traditional marketing channels and forcing themselves to be ultra creative, they were able to turn Dropbox into a massive company at an arguably faster pace than if they had spent money on media like television commercials or radio spots.[1]

Not only did Dropbox successfully explode their user growth, but they also built a very strong brand. They built a strong brand because the friend-to-friend referrals made it so that people had a higher regard and trust for the Dropbox brand than if Dropbox had introduced themselves to the consumer through traditional marketing methods. The growth engine that Dropbox used to grow has helped poise them for long-term success as a company.

CHAPTER 7
TRACTION LEADS TO GROWTH

Succeeding in business is all about making your product and company gain traction. If you create something with the "if we build it, they will come" mentality, it's going to be virtually impossible to make a successful business. You need to change that mentality to, "if we build it, we need to find out how to make people love us, and then they will come (and stay!)." Embracing the latter mentality will help you come up with ways to generate traction and watch significant growth begin to happen. If you don't think about how you're going to get your product in front of your target customers, you're likely not creating a business that can be successful.

Traction is pre-growth, and growth is what transforms an idea into a full-fledged business. A common mistake that founders of companies make is ignoring the ways they can grow their business early on by focusing too much on their product. If you think about creative ways to make people familiar with you and strongly believe in your product and brand early on, you're much more likely to create a business that skyrockets to success.

Unfortunately, it's almost impossible to predict which growth tactics will help you begin to see traction, but the experimentation is what makes building a business fun. To find traction, you need to turn yourself into an idea machine and rapidly test out your countless ideas to see if any of them are worth scaling. Growing a business by experimentation means that you get to understand your customers on a uniquely deep level because you see data and conversations happening about your company from the very beginning, and, if the business you're creating doesn't work out, you've now learned things that will help you create successful businesses in the future.

A great way to start thinking about how you will build traction is to start with a quote from economist and Harvard Business School professor Theodore Levitt: "People don't want to buy a quarter-inch drill. They want a quarter-inch hole[1]." Your target audience doesn't care about your product, they care about the outcome of your product and they will only buy or use a product because the product will help them achieve their desired goal.

Your product can help people achieve their desired goal by being better than a competitor's product. That's why the first step to finding traction is to identify weaknesses in your industry. When you find a weakness that you can exploit, you should take advantage and highlight how your product does it better than a competitor's product. You need to position yourself as a better solution than your competition.

Theodore Levitt elaborates on this notion brilliantly: "The marketing imagination is the starting point of success in marketing. It is distinguished from other forms of imagination by the unique insights it brings to understanding customers, their problems, and the means to capture their attention and their custom. By asserting that people don't buy things but buy solutions to problems, the marketing imagination makes an inspired leap from the obvious to the meaningful[1]."

Levitt continues this notion: "To differentiate an offering effectively requires knowing what drives and attracts customers. It requires knowing how customers differ from one another and how those differences can be clustered into commercially meaningful segments[1]."

Levitt is saying that to begin finding traction for your business, you need to spend time thinking about what drives your target customers and examine the other options besides yours that are available to these customers. When you know what drives your target customers and understand your competitors, you can begin focusing on coming up with ways that your business can gain traction.

You start to think about ways to drive traction by focusing on differentiation, providing a product or service better than a competitor, and then getting and keeping customers. These thoughts are the essence of your strategic traction plan, and by understanding those things you will be able to create a simple, yet elaborate, strategy. You can probably craft a marketing strategy that is just a few sentences long if you have a firm grasp on those things, and smart simplicity is the key to marketing success.

If you can't explain your marketing strategy in a few sentences, it's probably too complicated. Once you are able to whittle your thoughts down to a few sentences, you can focus on finding marketing channels that will help you find early traction for your product. When you are able to find early traction for your product, you've successfully set your growth engine in motion.

To begin your quest for traction, after you've spent time figuring out what truly differentiates your product, there are various methods for discovering the right traction channels to grow your business that you should be trying. These include: building an amazing product that delights users, clearly defining your goals, not only focusing on marketing activities that scale, and understanding your analytics.

1. <u>Build an amazing product</u>. If your product doesn't
   delight people, it's going to be hard to get people to

like it enough to share it with other people. If your product is bad, nobody will want to use it, let alone share it.

2. <u>Clearly define your big picture goal and break it down</u>. When crafting your traction strategy, clearly define your big picture goal. Perhaps your goal is to turn your business into a full-time job. That's a big goal, which is why it is a great idea to break down your bigger goal into smaller goals to make the bigger goal feel more achievable. This means asking yourself questions like, "How many customers per week do we need?" or "Do we think adding x feature will help us get more users?" or "Does integrating with another service make it easier for us to grow faster?"

3. <u>Don't only focus on things that scale</u>. This might sound counterintuitive, but not everything you do to early on to find your initial traction needs to be scalable. An example of a company that found their traction channel doing something that doesn't scale well is Tinder. Tinder is an online dating app that was able to break the taboo of young people using online dating tools, and they were able to do this in

a cost efficient way. When Tinder started, the founders hosted parties at USC where the only way you were allowed to get into the parties was by downloading the app. Tinder quickly grew, and, whether it was intentional or not, the high concentration of Tinder users at one school really helped the app explode in popularity. A dense area of app users meant that there was a community talking about the app and inevitably bringing it to other campuses. Sean Rad, a founder of Tinder, explained: "It happened around January. We had been picking up on college campuses, then everyone went home and told their cousins and older brothers and friends about it, and all of a sudden Tinder started growing like a virus[2]." The parties that Tinder threw weren't scalable, but the outcome of the parties worked to their advantage and helped the app skyrocket in popularity. Doing things that don't scale can be one of the easiest ways to drive organic growth because often the things that don't scale are the most personal experiences and get people talking about you.

4. <u>Understand your analytics</u>. If you don't understand your analytics, you won't be able to understand the

data points that help paint a picture of how people are interacting with your product and your marketing. By understanding your analytics, you will be able to figure out which traffic sources are driving the most growth, which type(s) of blog content generates the most sign ups, know if people are having a hard time converting on mobile, which landing pages convert best, and more. When you understand the data behind your business, you will identify items that are having a negative impact on your business, which means you can quickly correct the course by adjusting those items. Getting a firm grasp on your data can result in immediately noticeable growth results.

You will be able to find your traction when you've achieved product-market fit within a certain audience. Product-market fit means that you've hit a point where a significant amount, about 40% or more, of your users tell you that they would be very disappointed if they could no longer use your product[3]. Two ways that you can increase your likeliness of finding product-market fit include: rewarding users and using stronger brands to your advantage.

1. Reward users for inviting others. Rewarding users for inviting others is exactly what Dropbox did, and was their successful growth traction channel. This is a particular good channel to explore if there is little cost to you for giving away free product because it means you won't have to spend money on advertising, while benefiting from the power of friends and family referring each other to your product. To find out how to reward your users for inviting others, you should identify one value on your site that is most important to your users and give them the tools to increase that value. If you have a web hosting company, you might reward people with a free month of hosting for each referral sign up, or in Dropbox's case, give people free storage space when their referral begins using Dropbox.

2. Use other brands to your advantage. You can use other stronger brands to grow your brand. This means finding an aspect of your product that will benefit a bigger brand and set up partnerships with these brands. Forming partnerships can be

surprisingly easy since bigger companies often have dedicated business development teams who exist to create relationships between companies. However, there is another route you can take besides creating formal business development deals with bigger brands: create an API that bigger (or smaller) brands can leverage. An API effectively grants one piece of software the resources and/or data of another's by allowing communication and interaction between programs. By creating a useful API with your product, you can encourage other companies to partner with you and leverage your resources, which will introduce your brand to the users of another product.

These two things will help you find product-market fit because they will allow your users to associate your brand with their friends and family who referred them and also with bigger brands that they trust more than yours. If users come to your product from these strong referral sources, they're going be particularly disappointed to see your product no longer exist.

A common theme that is appearing in our discussion about traction is retention. Finding traction comes down to retaining users, and if you can't retain users, you're wasting your time focusing on the top of the growth funnel. The only way to know if your marketing tactics are effectively allowing you to retain users is if you constantly track how your users engage with your product. This means tracking your growth on a monthly or even weekly basis. Understanding your growth means that you can most accurately make decisions on which marketing effects your business faster. Understanding your growth doesn't only mean looking at views to your website or a user count, but understanding the value of the users that you're retaining. If you don't know your cost per acquisition (CPA) or lifetime value (LTV) of each user, how do you really know if your marketing is working? You shouldn't be spending a dollar more getting new users than they'll be worth over their life as a customer. To calculate LTV, you need to have a vast array of data on how users engage and stay on your site. Calculating lifetime value can be extremely difficult, so it's not something that we are going to elaborate on in this book. Just remember that understanding lifetime value and your cost to acquire a new user are vital to understanding your marketing efforts because you don't want to gain traction that is causing you to build a company that will just lose money. We also recommend that if you are a startup, your payback period for what you're paying to acquire a new customer be around just three months so that you can see positive cash flow growth at an early stage.

This chapter on traction has been slightly scattered in thought about how to begin finding your traction channel, but that is symbolic of the difficult task you face when trying to find the right traction channel(s) for your business. The hunt for traction is one of the most exhilarating parts of growth hacking, and the hunt requires you to scatter your thoughts to find success. Once you find the traction channel that works best for your business, you can focus and flip the switch to go from finding traction to creating sustainable long-term growth. Most companies find most of their growth from a single channel, so focusing on the channel that works for you will allow you to craft your growth machine and optimize it to fuel the rate at which your business grows.

CHAPTER 8
TRACTION AND GROWTH AREN'T THE SAME

Traction and growth are not quite the same thing. Traction comes before growth and traction is something that lets you discover how you should be spending your time marketing your product. When you start to see certain marketing channels generate traction for your business, you can focus on the tactics that make you grow most efficiently. Brian Balfour, VP of Growth at HubSpot, says that, "The traction phrase is where more startups are[1]." The goal of a startup is to move past the traction phase to the growth stage. To move into growth phase, you need to begin seeing user retention, the amount of new people using your product begin to steadily increase, and begin noticing that a lot of the traction is being driven by just one or a few marketing channels. The patterns of success that you begin to see during the traction stage means that you can hone in on the things that are driving your key metrics forward and optimize your marketing for the channels that drive the most growth. Optimizing your marketing for the channels that drive the most growth means experimenting with different messaging on these channels and also tinkering with the user onboarding process that people from these channels receive. Optimizing your marketing doesn't mean wasting your time on slight word changes to your website, changing the size or color of buttons, or doing tons of A/B tests. Optimizing your marketing means focusing on making big changes to make big discoveries that uncover big opportunities.

Focus on making big discoveries while optimizing by trying out big changes in messaging, user flow, and even at whom you're targeting your marketing. Don't get caught in the trap of focusing on micro-optimizations such as button colors, slight word tweaks, etc. There are certainly cases where tiny tweaks have lead to big results, but these cases of success from slight tweaks are more the outlier rather than the norm. Big changes will lead to big gains on the knowledge front, and your goal when optimizing the channels that are helping you begin to see real growth results is to make big discoveries, not little ones.

With an understanding of what's driving traction for you, you can now begin to think of ways to harness your lessons from the traction stage. You're ready to take the lessons learned from the traction stage of growing a business and start driving long-term sustainable growth. It's time to focus on your growth rate and making your growth rate move up and to the right faster.

CHAPTER 9
FINDING YOUR GROWTH MACHINE

Finding your growth machine can be very difficult. However, with the right mindset and understanding of your current users you can have that "aha" marketing moment where you discover exactly what is going to trigger monumental growth. Spotify figured out that by integrating with Facebook they could make people familiar with their brand and onboard users quickly, Uber used a combination of local partnerships and a viral referral program to grow, and Airbnb managed to piggyback off Craigslist to accelerate its growth.

While the untraditional marketing tactics that

worked for Spotify, Uber, and Airbnb won't necessarily for you, they're still good success cases to think about. Coming up with ways to evolve previously successful ideas can help you find your growth machine. To learn about evolving previously successful growth hacks to find your growth machine, we are going to take a look at three products: Hotmail, Gmail, and Mailbox.

Hotmail:

Hotmail launched back in 1996, and was able to get 20,000 users pretty quickly. At around this time, an early investor in Hotmail had an idea that he believed would accelerate their growth. He suggested that at the bottom of each email, they place a small advertisement for Hotmail. The advertisement was a line of text that read "Get Your Free Email at Hotmail." That's it— a simple little line of text that made it so that when users emailed friends and family they would promote their usage of Hotmail. Within 6 months of adding this line of text, the Hotmail user base exploded to over 1 million users. To put that into context, the entire Internet had just 36 million users the year that this explosive growth happened. That means almost 3% of the entire Internet was using Hotmail[1].

Gmail:

Fast-forward to eight years after Hotmail found its growth engine, and the Internet meets Gmail for the first time. Gmail was a big step forward for the Internet because of two key features: 1GB of free space (which was a lot at the time!) and they had a fantastic email search tool. Gmail was released in a very limited beta, with an invite system, which made it feel like a highly exclusive product. The limited beta of Gmail gave early Gmail users the option to invite friends, but invites were surprisingly hard to come by. The demand was so high for Gmail invites that they were actually being sold on eBay for over $100. The more people that created Gmail accounts and became users, the more product invites that became available, so eventually it became easy to create a Gmail account. The combination of a great product and the scarcity of invites fueled the rapid growth of Gmail. By mid-2012, eight years after Gmail was released, it had over 425 million users[1].

Gmail was a slightly evolved version of the Hotmail program, but instead of having a message along the lines of "Get Your Free Email at Hotmail,"

Gmail spread the word with the *@gmail.com* portion of the email address. The *@gmail.com* portion of the email address represented status and exclusivity, which made every email sent from an *@gmail.com* account promote the Gmail product. You saw your friends, family, and coworkers using the elusive and exclusive Gmail product, and you asked them to invite you so you could be part of the Gmail user club.

Mailbox:

The final mail program we are going to look at is Mailbox. Mailbox launched in early 2013, and used an invite system to achieve their monumental growth. However, Mailbox differed from Gmail and Hotmail because it used existing email services instead of creating a new one. Mailbox was simply a tool for better managing your emails and added new useful features to email platforms that already existed. The creatively crafted reservation system that Mailbox came up with is most likely the defining thing that the product and marketing team did to grow Mailbox into a major product. The Mailbox invite system was effectively an evolved version of the Gmail invite system because beyond the exclusivity aspect of a viral invite program, they also required everybody on the list to download the app to get a spot in line. Once a person downloaded the app, they would have the option to either enter in their invite code or claim their spot in line. By requiring users to install the app, Mailbox made user activation much more likely to happen once a person received their invite code. Over 800,000 people joined the Mailbox waitlist in just about one month, and Dropbox took notice. Dropbox acquired Mailbox for around $100 million in cash and stock[2]. And, just like Hotmail, Mailbox had a little "Sent from Mailbox" message at the bottom of every email to help raise awareness of their app.

What Hotmail, Gmail, and Mailbox have in common:

Hotmail, Gmail, and Mailbox all have one defining feature in the methods they used to grow: they used untraditional marketing tactics that cost them almost no money to implement. They found their breakthrough marketing success by ditching traditional marketing tactics, like buying television commercials, and came up with simple, yet brilliant, ways to activate their current users.

These three companies display the essence of great growth hacking. They found their growth machine and took full advantage of the opportunities that they had discovered. There is nothing magical about what these companies did besides identify unique growth opportunities and pounce on them. They also built their growth machines using both new and old tactics. They took growth tactics that had worked for a similar company and then focused their energy on developing reliable user acquisitions methods for themselves.

Crafting your growth engine: the growth hacking process

Before discussing how to craft your growth engine, it's important to take a step back and remember what makes up the growth hacker process.

In a nutshell, this is the growth hacker process:

1. Define yours goals.
2. Track your goals.
3. Take advantage of your strengths.
4. Experiment and optimize.
5. Repeat.

Define your goals: Great growth hacking only happens when you have focused smaller goals. We know that huge overall growth is the overarching goal of a growth hacker, but a narrow focus means that you will be able to work and craft your strategy in a more agile way and learn from your experiments much more quickly. You'll have better results by focusing on smaller goals because a lot of small wins add up to big growth.

Track your goals: You're wasting your time if you aren't taking the time to track your goals. This means using tools like Google Analytics to track traffic and other useful metrics. If you aren't using analytics to track your goals, your goals are meaningless. This is because you don't have the ability to understand if your goals are being reached. In addition, analytics gives you invaluable data that can help you decide if you need to change your goals. One of the biggest bonuses to having great data tracking is that you can understand how your growth marketing tactics are impacting your business over time. It's pretty rewarding to be able to look back at months or years worth of data and see how your marketing efforts are helping a business grow.

Take advantage of your strengths: It's pretty common for a marketer to try to come up with new ways to grow their business and accidentally disregard evaluating what's already working for her or him. Every company has strengths that can be leveraged to drive growth, so make sure you're evaluating what you are already doing to see if there's something you should be scaling or evolving. For example, if your company already has a large email list, why would you pour extra effort into trying to grow your social media following? Use your energy to come up with creative ways to leverage your existing large email list and put the audience that you already have to use.

Experiment and optimize: When you think that you've uncovered a good growth opportunity, it's time to experiment. Try out your hunch and see if there are any signs of traction. If you see traction you should consider ways to improve on your original results and then scale that effort. Experimentation is the quickest way to make meaningful learnings, so take time to focus on both failed experiments and successful experiments. By addressing why you think something failed, in addition to why something was successful, you can make sure you avoid consistently making the same marketing mistakes. When something fails, you should be asking yourself questions along the lines of: "Why do I think this failed? How could I have done the experiment better? Was my experiment focused enough on my smaller goal?" It's also vital to not be discouraged by initial results from experimentation. If something doesn't go as expected, think of that as a positive because you've made a valuable learning that will help you grow your business better, faster, and stronger.

Repeat: Set new goals, optimize the way you track goals, and continue experimenting. The more you repeat the growth hacker process, the more you'll learn and the more efficient you'll get at growing businesses faster.

To close out this chapter on finding your growth machine, we are going to examine the insights of David Ogilvy. David Ogilvy was an advertising wizard. He moved from Great Britain to New York

City to become the King of Madison Avenue. He became the King by creating some of the most iconic and successful advertising campaigns of all time. What's arguably just as impressive is that his marketing and advertising strategies, which he crafted from the '60s through the '80s, were so thought provoking that they can still be applied to products and services today.

The following quotes from Ogilvy will help you think about your product and perhaps lead to that "aha" marketing moment that helps you find your growth machine:

1. *"In the modern world of business, it is useless to be a creative, original thinker unless you can also sell what you create."* Just because you have a great product or service doesn't mean that it's going to knock it out of the ballpark sales-wise. You need to take the product or service and market it in a way that reaches and excites your target audience. Think about what you're marketing and constantly reexamine the motivations behind the messages you're sending out about the product or service you're trying to sell.

2. *"Talent, I believe, is most likely to be found among nonconformists, dissenters, and rebels."* Ogilvy was reminding people to think different. If you think like everybody else, you're just going to have the same results as everybody else. By thinking differently, you will find distinctive opportunities to successfully differentiate your product from your competitors.

3. *"If you're trying to persuade people to do something, or buy something, it seems to me you should use their language, the language they use every day, the language in which they think. We try to write in the vernacular."* This is a reminder from Ogilvy to know your audience. If you don't know your audience, you won't be able to speak to them in a convincing or personalized way. Speak your audience's language.

4. *"People who ignore research are as dangerous as generals who ignore decodes of enemy signals."* This was an Ogilvy way of saying that you need to do your research and then apply what you've learned to your marketing strategy. You should be

shaping your decisions based on thoughtful and informative research.

5. *"Never stop testing, and your advertising will never stop improving."* Keep experimenting, learn from every experiment, and apply what you've learned to a new experiment. It seems like intuitive advice, but it's easy to fall into a pattern of doing what you know and not experimenting with your marketing tactics.

6. *"Do not ... address your readers as though they were gathered together in a stadium. When people read your copy, they are alone. Pretend you are writing to each of them a letter on behalf of your client."* The master of advertising believed that it is vitally important to remember you're most often talking to an individual in marketing messages, not a group of people. If you remember this, it should help you connect with customers on a more personal level.

7. *"Don't bunt. Aim out of the ballpark. Aim for the company of immortals."* Ogilvy was a strong believer in not aiming for small achievements, but rather aiming as high as possible. He also believed

that every time you make a goal, make it (at least) a little bigger than your last goal.

The "don't bunt" ideology from David Ogilvy perfectly summarizes the essence of a growth hacker. A growth hacker is doing focused experiments with the ultimate goal of driving big growth. A growth hacker is aiming out of the park, and when a growth hacker successfully knocks it out of the park we see companies like Airbnb, Dropbox, and Mailbox achieve monumental growth at a rapid pace.

CHAPTER 10
COMMON GROWTH TACTICS

In the previous chapters, we've identified some growth hacking successes, talked about ways to hunt down traction, and also suggested that you look for ways that other companies have been successful at igniting growth and altering their successful strategies to match your audience and goals. This is why the logical next step in our discussion on growth hacking is to identify some ways you can leverage common growth marketing tactics to find your growth machine and build a business poised for long-term success. The growth tactics that we are going to focus on in this chapter include: viral marketing, search engine optimization, email marketing, unconventional PR, and event marketing. These are five fantastic growth marketing tactics to focus on because they are relatively easy to implement and have the potential positively impact your business in a huge way.

Viral marketing: The term viral marketing is thrown around a lot, but most people don't really have a fundamental understanding of what the term means. They simply assume that it means that a website or video gets a million views overnight. In reality, something doesn't need to get an insane amount of views to become a viral marketing success. For something to "go viral," you just need one user to refer at least one additional user. That's it. If one person refers just one more person and this chain of referral continues, you'll start to see accelerated growth.

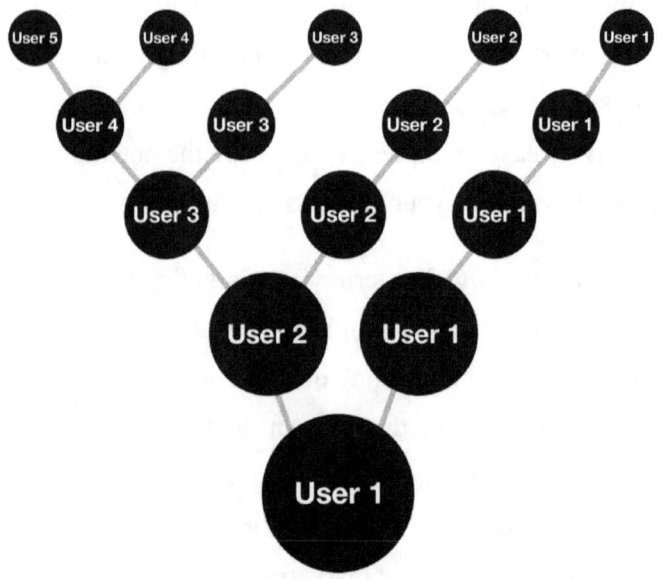

By focusing on creating ways to get one person to refer just one other person, you make the task of making a product "go viral" a whole lot less daunting and will see your product growth accelerate and spread. When crafting your viral strategy, focus on a small referral engine instead of creating a strategy that aims to get millions of views overnight, since overnight success is highly unlikely.

It is important to engineer virality into your product because just having a great product won't lead to a viral marketing home run. LinkedIn is a great example of a company that has built a viral loop into their product, and you probably don't even realize that they've done it when you're using it. The viral loop that LinkedIn has engineered accomplishes three things: it introduces visitors to their product, it does a great job introducing visitors to its product features and benefits, and then it converts visitors to users efficiently. LinkedIn only has value for these new users if they have a network, so it gives you the tools you need to find people that you know on the network, or invite people that you think should be on it. LinkedIn makes it easy to build and catalogue your professional network the moment you convert from visitor to user. LinkedIn uses the power of social networks to bring in and retain users.

LinkedIn was able to overcome early product adoption challenges and find traction by focusing on the tech community of the Silicon Valley area. The LinkedIn founders all had a powerful Bay Area network and following from being extremely successful at their previous companies, and they used this to their advantage. Reid Hoffman, a founder of LinkedIn explains: "We started slowly in the first few days because we wanted to make sure the systems worked. I think the 13 people associated with the company invited 112 people[1]." These initial users were also successful themselves, which made LinkedIn even more appealing to join. By having successful Silicon Valley players join the network, they made LinkedIn a product that everybody wanted to join because they saw opportunities to make meaningful business connections and meet potential investors. After the tech scene adopted LinkedIn, the network effect naturally started happening. People outside of the tech world began joining LinkedIn and the site became a place for people across all industries to rekindle old business relationships and form new ones. LinkedIn did a brilliant job forming their initial viral strategy and also proved that your viral strategy doesn't need to be super elaborate and complex.

LinkedIn showed us that creating your viral strategy starts with simply looking at your users. You need to understand your current users and what makes them users of your products and ask yourself: "What attracted these initial users to your product? What keeps these users coming back? Do these users already tell other people about your product?" If you don't know the answer to one, or all, of these questions, you should just ask some of your users and find the answers out. Ask your most loyal users what brings them back, and see if they're referring people or find out why they aren't referring people. After speaking to your loyal customers and answering these questions, you probably have an idea for a feature to focus on improving. Take these learnings and your idea for feature aspects that you believe will increase sharing and experiment like crazy. However, remember to not just experiment and toss ideas out, but to also take notes and learn from what you're doing. People love transparent companies, so you could even write blog posts on what you're trying out and what you're learning and give your users a window into the inner workings of your company.

Buffer is an example of a company that has done being transparent brilliantly, to the most extreme degree. Buffer posts information on employee equity, employee salaries, revenue, explains to customers what each cent of every purchase goes towards, shares fundraising updates, what books employees are reading, and even goes as far as making every email sent public within their team. There are effectively no secrets at Buffer, and transparency has been a key growth tactic driving Buffer's ascent to success since it has made people talk about their company, a lot. Transparency doesn't just lead to highly sharable content, but it's a great viral marketing tactic that helps create extremely loyal customers.

When you think about crafting your viral marketing strategy, you need to make sure you're setting goals for your efforts. Without goals, you have nothing to strive for. You have a meaningless company going in random directions. Set your goals and immediately lay out a dashboard with how you'll measure your goals. By creating a dashboard and immediately measuring the goals associated with your experiments, you can easily visualize and understand what you're doing.

After running a handful of experiments, you're likely to start to see usage and patterns in how people interact with your site. Just because a pattern arises doesn't mean you're golden though. Your pattern may help you notice that there are too many steps that a user needs to take to accomplish certain actions, which means you can now take the time to figure out how to reduce steps. When you make it as easy as possible for users to accomplish your growth goals, you're much closer to having a product that has the ability to achieve virality.

Unconventional PR: The PR industry is an interesting one. It's tremendously difficult to find a great agency that doesn't just charge you for a bunch of promises and ends up delivering little to no results. That's why the value of turning to unconventional PR methods is a great growth tactic. Unconventional PR is almost anything that doesn't involve sending out boring press releases. Unconventional PR is using unorthodox methods of getting the press to notice you and your company.

The "king" of unconventional PR is probably Richard Branson. He's a master of carrying out brilliant and unorthodox marketing stunts that help his businesses get massive amounts of press. Branson once donned a wedding dress for the launch of the new Virgin Brides bridal store. Back when (the now non-existent) venture launched in 1996, Richard Branson worked his magic to get the new company press. He shaved off his well-known beard and put on a $10,000 wedding dress. This simple media stunt amassed lots of exposure in newspapers and magazine and also helped further grow the Virgin brand. The Virgin brand benefits from stunts like this because it humanizes the brand, while also selling the idea that business doesn't always need to be serious. A humanized, offbeat, and fun brand is what has made Virgin so successful, and Richard Branson continues doing publicity stunts like this to help his brand stay strong.

You can try throwing on a wedding dress to get press, but, unless you're Mark Zuckerberg, Bill Gates, or Richard Branson, you're probably not going to get much press attention for doing that. Big names don't need to spend too much time engineering their unconventional PR tactics because they automatically make headlines when they do odd things. This means you need to strategize and meticulously engineer your publicity plan to help you go from relative anonymity to wündercompany. As an example of a great startup publicity stunt, we will examine the story of Lifelock.

Lifelock is an online identity protection tool. The company offers security services and tools that help protect its customers against identity theft. Back in

2006, the United States met the LifeLock CEO. His name is Todd Davis and his Social Security number is 457-55-5462. Seriously, that's his real name and real Social Security number. LifeLock posted this information everywhere and challenged America to steal his identity. His information was in magazine advertisements, on television, on massive billboards, and all over the place. People took notice to the CEO of LifeLock posting his personal identity information everywhere and this led to massive amounts of press for LifeLock. LifeLock quickly zoomed past having one million customers because of all of the press this stunt accumulated. Today LifeLock is a publically traded company worth over $1 billion.

However, this story isn't all fairy tale and rainbows. In 2010, *WIRED* reported that Todd Davis had had his identity stolen 13 times since the campaign launched[2]. What's even worse is that LifeLock didn't even catch the identity theft and in most of the instances Davis only became aware of the identity theft incidences when collection agencies came to collect on fraudulent accounts opened under his name. The FTC also accused LifeLock of operating a scam. FTC Chairman Jon Leibowitz explained: "In truth, the protection they provided left such a large hole … that you could drive that truck through it," with the truck Leibowitz referring to being from a LifeLock TV ad that featured a truck painted with Davis's Social Security number driving around a city. Luckily for LifeLock, these incidents never really garnered too much press, so Davis' new identity theft problems never really led to consumers questioning the company's ability to actually protect them.

While that publicity stunt ended up being somewhat unethical, and the last thing this book is suggesting to do is unethical marketing, it still teaches us some important unconventional PR lessons. The most important lesson learned from the LifeLock stunt is that a great unconventional PR campaign has the ability to shift conversation, at scale, in a way that benefits a company significantly.

Email: Email marketing is a great growth tool. Most people only get a handful of messages in their inboxes each day, which means you can cut through all of the clutter filling people's Facebook newsfeed and Twitter stream to deliver them promotions and information on your brand in an extremely visible and efficient way.

However, to send out effective email marketing campaigns you need to collect email addresses. This means that you need to come up with creative and compelling places for people to hand over their email addresses to your company. If you have a blog, try putting an email list sign up form at the bottom of a blog post or put an email list opt-in on the blog sidebar. Another great tactic for collecting email addresses is to create premium content that can only be unlocked with an email list subscribe. HubSpot has done a phenomenal job at generating leads using premium content, specifically e-books, to drive their massive growth. The HubSpot tactic of offering free e-books in return for an email address is a particularly great growth tactic because in addition to collecting a lead, HubSpot is demonstrating their brand expertise by educating people. HubSpot is showing the value of their brand and helping readers at the same time, which means e-book readers are much more likely to use paid HubSpot products than if they had just stumbled on a generic landing page. People trust the HubSpot brand because of their e-books and content marketing strategy and it has paid off enormously. Right now, HubSpot has grown into a publicly traded company worth over $1.75 billion.

Once you've truly begun growing your email list, you need to come up with ways to turn non-customers into customers. By using email to improve your customer (and potential customer) engagement rate, it becomes easy to educate people on key features of a product. You already know that a person is interested in your product if they're on your email list, so product education is key to turning a reader into a customer or increasing the revenue current customers generate. You can educate people by coming up with a customer engagement lifecycle messaging strategy. This means that you create specific messaging for when a person opts-in to your email list (perhaps with different messaging depending on where an opt-in happens), a message that educate users on your product (but don't be too salesy!), and finally a meaningful message focused on customer appreciation when a person makes a purchase.

Having a great email marketing strategy will not just help you get new customers, but it will also help you retain current customers. For many companies, email is the single most effective customer retention tool that they have. A great example of this is with Facebook. When you're tagged in a photo, Facebook will send you an email letting you know that a friend added a photo of you. This email is a simple strategic move on Facebook's part to keep you active on their site and encourages you to click on a call-to-action that brings you back to the Facebook website.

A smart email marketing strategy will help you get new customers and keep current customers engaged, which will increase the revenue that your product generates.

Search Engine Optimization: Search engine optimization (SEO) is one of those things that people often talk about but often overlook. It's a simple tactic to put search engines to work for you and introduce new people to your products at almost no cost. The core of SEO marketing is creating a smart content strategy because a smart content strategy will help you attract the visitors that you want on your website. You need to be smart about the type of content you make, and the way you write it, because original content that is written well and optimized to promote certain keywords will rise to the top of search results.

When starting to shape your SEO strategy, it is a smart idea to think about keywords that will most effectively put you on the front page of search results. When coming up with your target keywords, keep in mind things like how if you're just starting a business, it's going to be extremely hard for you to conquer a term like, "marketing software." With this in mind you can try to think about terms, such as "marketing software for coffee shops," that will be easier to rank on the first page for. That's a slightly peculiar example, but you get the gist— a term like "marketing software for coffee shops" will be much less competitive than "marketing software."

If your content is supporting the keywords you want to win, the more likely you are to rank high. Links to your website are also important for increasing your rank. This means that you should have high quality content that you try to get linked to from bigger websites. In addition to the benefit of a bigger website subtly promoting your brand, having bigger websites link to you increases your credibility and makes search engines trust your content more. Making content that people want to link to is no easy feat though— you need to be particularly remarkable for people to want to share what you've written about. The previous example of Buffer being ultra transparent is also a fantastic example of remarkable content that people link to a lot. The unusual level of transparency at Buffer, which people love talking about online, is most likely why Buffer ranks higher than bigger companies like Hootsuite on Google for terms like, "social media scheduling."

SEO is made up of two components: links and content. Great content (that supports your focus keywords) generates more links to your website from other websites. When other websites link to your content, it increases your sites credibility and you rank higher.

Your business or startup probably won't fail because of a poorly executed or non-existent SEO strategy, but you will fail at effectively finding new customers in a very cost efficient manner that also boosts your brand reputation. Prioritizing content marketing is something that marketing teams should be doing if they want to boost the amount of new customers acquired at a low price.

Offline events: Another low price growth tactic is

sponsoring and participating in offline events. Big trade shows are typically a waste of time, and if there are booth numbers at an event you probably don't want to participate. It's extremely hard to stick out at large trade show, and if you can't stand out it's almost impossible for people to discover you. Sponsoring and participating in small to medium-sized offline events will be the easiest way for you to find traction at events.

In addition to being able to find traction at small events, they also give you the unique opportunity to talk to your target audience directly. The more of your target audience you talk to, the better you'll be able to craft your product to be something that they don't just want, but feel like they absolutely need. If your target customer doesn't respond well to your product, you'll be able to see this at events and correct the course of your company almost immediately.

The smaller to medium-sized events that are the easiest to succeed at are primarily meetups and hackathons. These small events allow you to do more than just place your logo in the face of participants, but actually form relationships. You know that an event was a success when you walk away with meaningful long-term relationships with your target audience. The more relationships you're able to form at events, the bigger your network becomes made up of people who want to see your product succeed.

You can easily find an existing meet up or event by browsing around a site like Meetup or Eventbrite. If you're lucky, you'll stumble across an opportunity that changes the course of your business.

A fantastic event success story is what the company behind the .CO domain name extension did to become well adopted. The company behind .CO became a global sponsor of Startup Weekend. If you're unaware of what Startup Weekend events are, they are hackathons to create a viable business in just 54 hours. There have now been over 1,500 Startup Weekend's in over 725 cities! The amount of events grew immensely fast and the .CO registry went along for the ride by sponsoring every event in every city. The sponsorship was simple: .CO provided every Startup Weekend participant access to their own .CO domain for free, for a year. This meant that each weekend, hundreds (if not thousands) of eager entrepreneurs and early adopters were registering a free .CO domain name for their ideas. This accomplished two things: it made early adopters feel comfortable using a domain extension that wasn't .COM, and also tied a fun experience to the .CO brand. The combination of .CO and Startup Weekend working together meant that .CO had become an aspirational and inspirational product. The usage of a .CO was tied to a great experience, which meant a person who had participated in a Startup Weekend was more likely to purchase and recommend a .CO in the future, and these early adopters of .CO were setting an example for the rest of the Internet by launching brilliant ideas on .CO domain names. The .CO domain name became widely used and was acquired by Neustar for $109 million[3]. It's safe to say that .CO's sponsorship of Startup Weekend is what showed .CO that they should focus on the startup community and sponsor tons of other startup events, and this focus on the startup community helped lead them to a 9-figure acquisition.

An event like Startup Weekend is effectively a mini-conference, except you miss out on the boring conference part and focus on actually getting stuff done. Startup Weekend is all about the idea of "no talk, all action," which perfectly summarizes why small events are such a good growth tactic. These types of small events can be cheap and easy ways to see if your target audience likes your product, while also helping you gain traction. Once you've found an event that helps you gain traction, scale your efforts at similar events. You know what works, so invest your time (and money) in showing value and supporting the people who can make your product successful.

While there are many other growth tactics out there, we decided to focus on viral marketing, unconventional PR, email marketing, search engine optimization, and offline events. We picked these five growth channels because they are some of the easiest to implement for the least amount of money. If you execute on one of these growth tactics well, there's no reason why you shouldn't see website traffic or sign ups for your product increase. All of these methods also let you build a community around your company and let you harness the power of customer evangelists. These five tactics let you demonstrate so much value to people that people want to talk about your business and share your product because they want to see you succeed.

CHAPTER 11
THE HACKER MENTALITY

We've now examined what it means to be a growth hacker, how to create a killer growth marketing strategy, the importance of community, the difference between traction and growth, why failure is important to be a successful growth hacker, and some common growth tactics. By now, you should be inspired and ready to tackle supercharging the growth of your business. However, while trying to craft a concise book, we ended up packing in a lot of information into not a lot of pages. That is why, to close out *Hacking Growth,* we are going to examine what the hacker mentality is and how you can use the hacker mindset to send your company into hyper-growth mode.

The original definition of a hacker does not revolve around the notion of writing mischievous code, but rather outlines a person who is an exceptionally creative builder and innovator. You are a hacker, and that's why you picked up this book. You picked up this book because you wanted a toolset to refine your way of innovating and you love conquering challenge after challenge. You most likely often feel like you have no idea what you're doing, but take comfort in the fact that visionary leaders like Steve Jobs or Elon Musk were once at this same point of not know what they were doing in their professional journeys. A hacker is drowning in a sea of knowledge and when everything clicks, they make big things happen.

Mark Zuckerberg summed up the hacker mentality perfectly in a letter to Facebook investors. He said, "The Hacker Way is an approach to building that involves continuous improvement and iteration. Hackers believe that something can always be better, and that nothing is ever complete[1]." Zuckerberg's explanation of what it means to be a hacker is a reminder that many people have faced the same business problem you're facing now, and it's your duty to reiterate on what has been done before and do it better. You need to test, tweak, and explore your creative and intellectual boundaries to make big discoveries.

By constantly tweaking and testing, while examining how other people have solved problems similar to yours, you are going to uncover where they could have solved their problem better. When you discover how somebody else could have done something better, and exploit his or her weaknesses, you become a disrupter.

Uber is a wonderful example of a company that thought like a hacker to be an industry disrupter. The founders of Uber identified weaknesses, inefficiencies, and acknowledged the unremarkable experience of getting a taxi. The founders figured out a way to make getting a hired car more reliable, easier, and fun. They built their simple, yet disruptive, product with a hacker mindset and baked their marketing strategy directly into their product.

When you can think like a hacker and create products with a marketing mindset, you can make amazing businesses. If you are part of an established business, or just getting a new company started, it's your responsibility to encourage the hacker mindset. You are a good employee or founder when you encourage the hacker mindset because it makes it a lot less likely that you will be disrupted. And, if you get disrupted, you're likely to be disrupting yourself because you will be able to more clearly see how the world is continuously changing and how your company needs to take certain actions to exploit change to fuel growth. When a company embraces the hacker mentality it is always one step ahead and won't miss out on opportunities to best adapt to a constantly changing world.

To be a great growth hacker, you need to be able to identify weaknesses and opportunities in the way things currently exist, and then pounce on the weaknesses and opportunities that you discover. You need to not accept things at face value and unleash your inner idea machine to constantly come up with hacks that will position you ahead of the competition. Find an opening to do something a little bit better than somebody else and come up with creative ways for your target audience to discover your product. Once somebody becomes a user of your product, create compelling reasons for them to talk about your product and make it easy for users share your product with their friends, family, and professional network.

If you build a great product and make it easy for people to talk about how great your product is, there is no reason why you can't build a great business.

Alex Kehr

ACKNOWLEDGMENTS

I was inspired to create this book after reading
Growth Hacker Marketing by Ryan Holiday and
Traction by Justin Mares and Gabriel Weinberg.
Both of these books undoubtedly influenced me
greatly, and I want to thank those three authors for
unknowingly nudge me to write my own book.

SOURCES

Below are the places and people who gave me various data and information, and also helped kick my brain into hyper drive.

Chapter 1

1: The 7 Ways Dropbox Hacked Growth to Become a $4 Billion Company
https://blog.kissmetrics.com/dropbox-hacked-growth/

2: How Referrals Built The $10 Billion Dropbox Empire
http://www.referralcandy.com/blog/referrals-built-dropbox-empire/

3: Sean Parker: Philanthropy for Hackers
http://www.wsj.com/articles/sean-parker-philanthropy-for-hackers-1435345787

Chapter 2

1: The Growth Hacker Conversion Funnel
http://www.quicksprout.com/the-definitive-guide-to-growth-hacking-chapter-4/

Chapter 3

1: Building Loyal Customers in the Information Age
http://knowledge.wharton.upenn.edu/article/hold-tweet-building-loyal-customers-information-age/

Chapter 4

1: How the Loyalty Loop is Replacing the Marketing Funnel
http://blog.generalassemb.ly/loyalty-loop-replacing-marketing-funnel/

Chapter 5

1: Creativity, Inc.: Overcoming the Unseen Forces That Stand in the Way of True Inspiration
By Ed Catmull. Published by Random House.

Chapter 6

1: Case Study: Dropbox Invites
http://jwegan.com/growth-hacking/case-study-dropbox-invites/

Chapter 7

1: The Marketing Imagination, by Theodore Levitt
http://rites-of-

passage.com/images/Levitt_TheMarketingImagination. pdf

2: How Tinder Is Winning the Mobile Dating Wars
http://www.inc.com/issie-lapowsky/how-tinder-is-

winning-the-mobile-dating-wars.html

3: The critical metrics for each stage of your SaaS business
http://andrewchen.co/the-critical-metrics-for-each-stage-of-your-saas-business-guest-post-by-lars-lofgren-of-kissmetrics/

Chapter 8

1: Traction vs Growth
http://www.coelevate.com/essays/traction-vs-growth

Chapter 9

1: How You Can Find The Next Big Growth Hack
http://www.natedesmond.com/how-you-can-find-the-next-big-growth-hack/

2: Meet the Man Who Sold a Month-Old App to Dropbox for $100M
http://www.wired.com/2013/05/gentry-underwood/

Chapter 10

1: LinkedIn's startup story: Connecting the business world
http://money.cnn.com/2009/06/02/smallbusiness/linkedin_startup_story.smb/index.htm

2: LifeLock's CEO Identify Stolen 13 Times
http://www.wired.com/2010/05/lifelock-identity-theft/

3: Neustar acquires .CO for $109 million
http://domainnamewire.com/2014/03/20/breaking-neustar-acquires-co-for-109-million/

Chapter 11

1: SEC Form S-1 Registration Statement, Facebook
*http://www.sec.gov/Archives/edgar/data/1326801/0001
19312512034517/d287954ds1.htm*

ABOUT THE AUTHOR

Alex Kehr was born in Santa Monica, California and studied Advertising at the University of Colorado Boulder. He is a marketing strategist who has been building websites and businesses online since he was only nine years old. He, and his online projects, have been written about in numerous publications, including: *The New York Times*, *WIRED*, *NY Daily News*, and many others.

</book>

www.ingramcontent.com/pod-product-compliance
Lightning Source LLC
Chambersburg PA
CBHW070813180526
45168CB00002B/603